THE
POWER
OF POETRY

THE FUTURE · HOPE · POWER · IDENTITY · POLLUTION · BULLYING · DISCRIMINATION · DESTRUCTION · DISASTER · WAR · POVERTY · EQUALITY

Word Weavers

Edited By Debbie Killingworth

First published in Great Britain in 2023 by:

Young Writers
Remus House
Coltsfoot Drive
Peterborough
PE2 9BF
Telephone: 01733 890066
Website: www.youngwriters.co.uk

Printed and bound in the UK by BookPrintingUK
Website: www.bookprintinguk.com
YB0528DZ

FOREWORD

Since 1991, here at Young Writers we have celebrated the awesome power of creative writing, especially in young adults where it can serve as a vital method of expressing their emotions and views about the world around them. In every poem we see the effort and thought that each student published in this book has put into their work and by creating this anthology we hope to encourage them further with the ultimate goal of sparking a life-long love of writing.

Our latest competition for secondary school students, **The Power of Poetry,** challenged young writers to consider what was important to them and how to express that using the power of words. We wanted to give them a voice, the chance to express themselves freely and honestly, something which is so important for these young adults to feel confident and listened to. They could give an opinion, highlight an issue, consider a dilemma, impart advice or simply write about something they love. There were no restrictions on style or subject so you will find an anthology brimming with a variety of poetic styles and topics. We hope you find it as absorbing as we have.

We encourage young writers to express themselves and address subjects that matter to them, which sometimes means writing about sensitive or contentious topics. If you have been affected by any issues raised in this book, details on where to find help can be found at
www.youngwriters.co.uk/info/other/contact-lines

CONTENTS

Florence Marshall (11)	79
Denzel Cristian Cabaya Cerias (11)	80
Freya Twaite	81
Isla Saunders (11)	82
Aadi Patel (12)	83
Archie Maloney (11)	84
Emily Carter (11)	85
Jed Bentley (11)	86
Macey Bain (12)	87
Destiny Rayne Cicley Bevan (12)	88
Daisy Coulson (12)	89
Trinh Tran (11)	90
Lexie Ewart (11)	91
Kayleigh Swinton (11)	92
Jake Wray (11)	93
Jack Harness (11)	94
Morgan-Jay Barrow (12)	95

Berwick Academy, Spittal

Esmay Fairbairn (14)	96
Romilly Oliver (14)	98
Joseph Todd (14)	99
Alfie Wilson (15)	100
Craig Hiroz (14)	101
Maddie Ferrell (14)	102
Isabella McPherson (14)	103
Ruby Haldon (14)	104
Imogen Meakin (14)	105
Imogen Mitchell (14)	106
Emily Parsons (14)	107
William Gilchrist (14)	108
Heidi Scott (14)	109
Stuart Wakenshaw (14)	110

Brentside High School, Ealing

Sumedha Suntharalingam (15)	111
Fatimah Shah (15)	112
Mischa Nicolas (13)	115
Krishmit Singh (14)	116
Sharae Hay (12)	118
Myles Cayford (13)	119

Udaya Thapa (12)	120
Rudin Nika (13)	121
Mariya Kimura (13)	122
Elifnur Soysal (11)	123
Eloise Nateguy (11)	124
Maia Alves Da Silva (13)	125
Yasmin Gelle (13)	126
Olla Shawari (13)	127
Zahraa Ataya (11)	128
Ema Subert-Shikama (11)	129
Neameh Al-Talha (11)	130
Safiya Noor (11)	131
Daniel Malaeb (11)	132
Gurleen Kour (11)	133
Troy Mercan (11)	134
Zayn Ali (11)	135
Armstrong Sutharsan (11)	136
Redouane Boutiche (11)	137

Co-Op Academy Bebington, Wirral

Robert Bollans (12)	138
Maisie-Lea Allinson (12)	139
Amelia Frost (12)	140
Amy Guttenberg (12)	141
Kai Carress (12)	142
Adam Fletcher (12)	143
Blake Pinch (12)	144
Jake Devaney (12)	145
Jacob Williams (12)	146
Brodie Humphreys (12)	147
Zaniar Baktiar (12)	148
Toby Mccoy (12)	149
Aaron Minshull (12)	150
Jayden Davies (12)	151
Alfie Westmoreland-Rigg (12)	152
Luke Moran (13)	153
Blake Boardman (12)	154
Adam Call (12)	155
Luke Mansell (12)	156
Joey Blakeborough (12)	157
Havish Susanta Panda (12)	158
Harvey Wright (12)	159

Alex O'Hanlon (12)	160
Oliver Johnson (12)	161
Ryan Smith (12)	162
Leighton Burke (12)	163
Oliver Griffiths (12)	164
Austen Pedersen (12)	165
Lewis Knott (12)	166
Arron Mitchell (12)	167
Archie Carrigan (12)	168
Bryn Essam (12)	169
William Scott	170
Wentworth Smith (12)	171
Taylor Anderton (12)	172
Joel-Peter Maddocks (12)	173
Taylor Lewis (12)	174
Jack Graham (12)	175
Jack Johnson (12)	176
Owen Harvey (12)	177
Finley Edge (12)	178

North Cambridge Academy, Kings Hedges

Ilianna Cartwright (15)	179
Ella Fordham (13)	180
Emma Thomas (13)	182
Alvar Meyer zu Eissen (12)	184
Ruth Dawson (12)	185
Dasche Ryan (12)	186
Manon Turner (12)	187
Abby Ho (12)	188
Isaac Rayson (12)	189

THE
POEMS

Environment

E very person has a responsibility for the environment.

N ever drop plastic waste in the ocean.

V ery few people care about this situation, if you are one of these people then please listen to this message.

I t is our responsibility to not buy plastic bottles and straws or packaging.

R euse metal stuff or if you use plastic, reuse it then recycle it properly.

O ver your entire life you should be recycling stuff, if you don't know where you can do this, do some research.

N ever leave lights on, never drop litter, never waste plastic.

M y burning question is: do you want to live your life fully without having to worry?

E very person should get involved.

N ow you can enjoy your life.

T hank you for listening. I believe we can make a difference.

Lucy Woolford (13)

Amery Hill School, Amery Hill

Backwards

Backwards is what I think the world means.
Evolution is when we must evolve from our mistakes,
Change the way we look, walk, eat, hunt.
But, why is it that we are going one step forward and two
steps back?
Why is it that we are evolving backwards?
We all act like we are standard, but look around us...
There are polar bears dying of the swelling heat.
People must think we should take a seat,
That we should watch this happen around us,
Even though we are the people of the upcoming generation,
Who will lead the people and show us the right path.
Yet we are walking down the wrong footpath,
We have chosen leaders that aren't leading us.
Governments decide to ban plastic straws,
But what about the other flaws?
Protests, poems, songs and documentaries,
All using their voice to spread the word.
Some will sit but take it in,
Whilst others will hear it but will let it go out the other ear,
Not do anything to mend our planet that should last us a
lifetime.
Otherwise, we shall run out of time.
We need to take another look,
Start a new chapter in this book.
We need new leaders, new beginnings,

A fresh society that would fix everything that has been
going on for almost two hundred years!
Otherwise, we will be going backwards.
It's the money that politicians and governments want,
Because they are too blind to see these changes,
Because it's the money,
They think we as a lower class should have to listen to them,
Because they have the loudest voices,
But we can be loud too.
There will soon be no view,
No view of a fresh start,
No view of new generations,
And certainly no view of the tree outside your window... as
it'll be gone.
The world is evolving backwards.
We can change that,
We can change the way they see,
This is for a fresh, new upbringing of evolving.

Laeton Fawcett (13)

Amery Hill School, Amery Hill

These Poor Traffic Cones

Us traffic cones have been abused
Used for something we didn't choose to do
We get run over by a car
Then sent far
Along the road
What did we do to deserve this?
We're just like any animal: a mammal, reptile or a fish
We might just be a cone
The road is our home
And these cars don't care
They run us over
With brands like a Land Rover
Just stick to land
And you won't be caught with a red hand
For murder.

We don't ask for much
We don't take showers for hours and hours
Like you do
We don't need food and water
Like you do
We don't have a bed and a nighttime routine
Like you do
We don't ask for gifts or someone to give us a lift
Like you do

All we are are cones trying to stay in our home
Not like you.

All we ask for is respect
Not to vote for who you elect
Just respect
Us cones
Are manufactured
Then fractured
Along the road
We don't harm you
We live with you
Alongside you
We help you
Protect you
From a car crash.

Yet you don't spend money
It's quite funny
That we sit on the floor
You and your cars flatten us like a doormat
Buy a driving lesson
So you don't send us to heaven
We go to heaven, not hell
We do our job well
And all you do is murder us
You kill us with a car, bike, foot or bus.

Now see what you have just read
Do you now want to see another cone dead?
Use that brain in your head
And remember
We are just cones
Trying to live in our home
Along the road.

Gabriel Pease (13)
Amery Hill School, Amery Hill

Covid

In March 2020, Britain entered panic
Toilet rolls all disappeared, supermarkets manic
Boris Johnson announcements, stuck inside at home
Whilst we heard his boring voice all we did was moan.

Joe Wicks' home workouts were the absolute worst
Parents helping with your work, they were about to burst
Wearing masks when going out, longing to see friends
When would this pandemic meet a brilliant end?

2021 began, hope for a better future
Back to school in person, no meeting with a teacher
But suddenly it struck again
Inject yourself with bleach, huh?

A never-ending circle but now a common cold
Stories range from young ones all the way up to the old
We come from across the Earth, stand up and unite
Because Covid pandemic, we won't back down, instead we'll fight.

James Wren (13)
Amery Hill School, Amery Hill

I'm Okay

Okay? It's better than okay!
I finally got my own phone!
I'm literally going to explode!
I'm going to get Snapchat, TikTok, Instagram,
You name it, I'm getting it!

Oh my God! This filter makes me so much skinnier!
My photo already got ten likes!
OMG guys.

I have one hundred followers!
That's like, loads,
I don't even know some of them.

I love this photo my friend took,
It's so cute,
I'll post it right now!

I hope that people like it,
I love it so much!

Oh.

'Fat LOL', 'Why is she making that face?'
'Imagine still wearing that at our age!', 'Ugly'.
They're just joking,
They don't really think I look that bad,
I'll try again another time.

Okay, I'll post this one now,
I got some new clothes,
They must like this pic more,
I even dyed my hair because everyone knows,
Blonde is the best colour.

'OMG embarrassing, she actually thinks she looks good!'
'KYS'
Maybe they're right,
Maybe I'll never be good enough.

Kill yourself?
Really, that's what people think,
Okay? I don't think I'll ever be okay again.

Okay, okay, okay, okay, okay, okay, okay, okay,
If I keep saying it I'll be okay,

Probably...

Phoebe Hall (15)
Amery Hill School, Amery Hill

Cheaters

What do you know about cheaters?
How can you tell
If the man you love so much is behind your back cheating?
We are too scared to ask if he is cheating
We are far too scared of losing that person
People get cheated on all the time
But told it was our fault
When someone leaves they show the real person they are
But how?
How do we stop this betrayal that they portray
So we can have a better day?
Even though heartbreak and make you cry
And to the day you have to say goodbye
You think what was fake, what was real?

Some people are nice and some people lie
And don't understand that we are humans
Some people just let you down
Then let you down and let you down
But deep down inside
You try to fight through the tide of the heartbreak
And the stuff you put aside
But it never works
But you get broken and broken and broken again
Don't let anyone change you or define you

Stand up for your freedom
You can fight, you can fight
You can't flight.

Maybe you did
Maybe you lost
But in every heartbreak comes a lesson in life
And a hell of a good glow up
You learn from the past
But afraid for the future
But it is always today
So go out and live your life
Live for peace
Live for yourself
But especially don't let people control you.

Willow Veck (14)

Amery Hill School, Amery Hill

Seasonal Feelings

Winter:

When January hits,
And the weather is too cold,
Hail and rain spits.

The festive season collapses on us,
And jingling of bells creates tension,
The twenty-fifth Is all of the fuss.

When stockings are hung,
And families are buzzing,
Christmas carols are sung.

Summer:

When happiness arrives with the sun,
And exotic fruits are vivid,
Everyone is after fun.

When more hours make longer days,
And light engulfs the darkness,
Night is a shorter phase.

Spring:

When the trees are so green,
And joy is in the air,
Loads of butterflies are to be seen.

When friends and family are around,
We're all waiting for the chocolate to be found.

Autumn:

When the chill comes back,
And leaves cascade,
All you want is a snuggle and a snack.

When night elapses and it is so dark,
And companions frighten you,
You trick or treat in the park.

Evie Smith (11)
Amery Hill School, Amery Hill

The Mountain

I stand tall with a cap of snow,
I hear the rumbling thunder,
I see great powers crumble,
I make you fall before you reach your peak,
I question how long you survive,
I am the mountain.

I pretend to be benevolent,
I feel your feet on snow,
I touch the seas and the skies,
I worry about your success,
I cry when you die,
I am the mountain.

I understand your burning quest,
I say you need not climb,
I dream of your success,
I try to end your dreams,
I await your eventual end,
I am the mountain.

I make the black clouds above,
The ice like glass below,
I stole the dreams of those who came before you,
You will not have your day,
I am the mountain.

You may be strong in will,
But you will be made weak by time and fate,
You will yield,
And I will let you fall,
I am the mountain.

Daniel Williams (15)

Amery Hill School, Amery Hill

The Queen

Philip came to me today,
He told me he had something to show me,
And there I was, lying down in a bed,
Surrounded by my whole family,
My beautiful sons,
But my family were crying and holding my hand,
I was confused,
I asked Philip but he had no response,
He took my hand gently and walked me over to my family,
And all he said was, "Touch them on the shoulder,"
And that is what I did.

He then took me up this long stairway,
And at the top of it, I got given my crown,
But the people up here called it a halo?
The only difference up here was that everyone was wearing a crown,
I was the only one that felt out of place,
But Philip held my hand the whole way
And he told me everything was normal now,
I am now in a world full of kings and queens.

Khia Stubbs (14)
Amery Hill School, Amery Hill

A Changed World

Climate change has changed the world
It has made many animals die
It is not time just to relax and not time to thrive
Pollution is a worldwide problem that animals try to survive
Like the deer galloping up and high
It's like its running on the blue sky
But then it stopped and nearly died
There was a plastic bag on the tree
Most of them are free and got stuck on a tree
Please just stop littering or else I'll keep nagging
Hunters and poachers kill all the wildlife
Like the deer up and high, it's running on the blue sky
But then it stopped and nearly died
It's like someone wanted to say goodbye
They shot the deer and the deer died
Then the hunters said that was a good night.

Ryan Shankland (11)
Amery Hill School, Amery Hill

Stop Deforestation

S top deforestation because
T rees are being cut down every second
O ver half of the Amazon rainforest is already done
P eople are destroying it all.

D eforestation needs to stop
E veryone has a chance
F or animals should too
O n no other planet there are trees, so
R estore our losses for
E very second a tree falls, so
S top cutting down trees because
T rees help us to live
A nd animals' homes
T rees turn into our houses
I n fifty years the Amazon rainforest will be gone
O ur people cutting down trees bad, so
N ever cut a tree again.

Oliver Parratt (12)
Amery Hill School, Amery Hill

The Balloon Thief

Balloons drift to the sky,
When we let them go.
We often say our last goodbye,
While they're travelling nice and slow.

When they are out of sight,
Do they just disappear?
Or do they carry on their flight,
And stay up there all year?

Is there a balloon thief,
Who takes them for himself?
To everyone's disbelief,
He snatches them with stealth.

And hides them in his cloudy lair,
To add to his collection.
It would never cross his mind to share,
The fruits of his life's obsession.

Or does he have to start from scratch,
Every single day?
Because his lovely lady match,
Throws them all away!

Sophie Knapp (11)
Amery Hill School, Amery Hill

Smartphones

They are incredible,
So many features,
Calling, texting, photos, the World Wide Web,
All compacted into the palm of your hand,
You can connect with people,
Help you with your homework,
All in the palm of your hand,
They are amazing, truly amazing.

However, they are everywhere,
Literally everywhere,
You won't be able to walk anywhere,
To town, to school, to work,
Without seeing one,
They are addictive.

Social media,
Click me, swipe me, like me,
Glueing people to their screens,
As if they were possessed,
Not paying attention,
Lifeless, no physical communication.

All in the palm of your hand.

Ethan Viner (14)
Amery Hill School, Amery Hill

You Were Warned

I miss the times when the flowers bloomed
In a bright array of pinks, yellows and blues,
I miss the times when the smell of springtime filled the air
And the tall, green trees swayed in the breeze.

But now, the sky stays ominous black and the world feels doomed,
The flowers droop and rot into the ground,
The air is clogged with ash,
Trying to ensnare all light and life from the already broken world.

Is this where you want your child to live, in a world entombed?
In a world of pain and suffering?
If not then help make a change,
It doesn't have to be a big task,
Just do your part,
So that your child can live in a world of beauty.

Sam Gale (14)
Amery Hill School, Amery Hill

The World Is Your Canvas!

E legant trees that lurk over us and watch our every move
N oisy waterfalls cascading all over our land
V egetation and growth help us live
I mpeccable beauty that can't be replaced
R unning the race of every day keeps life growing
O n each day, new life soon emerges to start their life
N ot only helping us live, helping us grow a grand, green
world of beauty
M ountains that reach as high as the sky, touching the
candyfloss clouds
E ndless mountains of money don't always mean
everything in life
N ature is free and puts a new prospect of life in our world
T he world is your canvas!

Isabelle Cooke (11)

Amery Hill School, Amery Hill

The Black And Big Hoodie

Whose hoodie is that? I think I know.
Its owner is quite sad though.
She is unhappy; her brain filled with woe.
I watch her pace. She cries for help inside.
She gives her hoodie a shake,
She screams; she thinks she is a mistake.
I cry for her, but she walks away,
The only other sounds that break,
Are the distant waves and birds awake.
The hoodie is black, big and deep,
But she has secrets to keep,
Tormented with nightmares she never sleeps.
Revenge is a promise a girl should keep.
She rose from bed,
With thoughts of violence in her head,
She sees rage,
She sees red,
Everyone that hurt her should have fled.

Amy Wright (14)
Amery Hill School, Amery Hill

My Beautiful Girl

Roses are red,
Violets are blue,
Flowers are beautiful,
And so are you.

Orchids are white,
Ghost ones are rare,
The appearance is wavy,
And so is your hair.

Magnolia grows,
With buds like eggs,
A face is smooth,
And so are your legs.

Sunflowers reach,
Up to the skies,
The thought is lustful,
And so are your eyes.

Foxgloves in hedges,
Surround the farms,
Your smile is gracious,
And so are your arms.

Daisies are pretty,
Daffodils have style,

My lights are illuminating,
And so is your smile.

Willow Vallery (14)
Amery Hill School, Amery Hill

Horses

Horses, the gorgeous creatures,
Rearing and neighing for food,
They are the ones that care,
The ones that love,
The ones that are wild and free.

They buck and they whinny,
Pleading to you.
Can I have a carrot?
Or I will throw a shoe.

They trot and they canter,
On cold and hot days,
No matter the cost,
They will ride for you.

They gallop and stride,
Looking mighty and proud,
They run in the wind,
Wild and free as one can be.

As you can see,
They are creatures like us,
So, never hurt them,
Or they will come running back.

Olivia Saker (12)
Amery Hill School, Amery Hill

My Favourites Box

Inspired by 'Magic Box' by Kit Wright

I will put in my box...
The hum of a hummingbird,
The sound of a sneaky snake slithering,
A bumble bee buzzing.

I will put in my box...
A herd of hungry cows,
Water falling between rocks,
People thoughtfully waving from a speedy train.

I will put in my box...
The taste of a freshly grown strawberry,
The smell of lots of different coloured daisies,
The smell of pizza cooking in the oven.

I will put in my box...
A wizard riding a venomous condor,
A flower made to look like a monkey face,
A group of poisoned dart frogs chilling on lily pads.

Bethany Webster (11)
Amery Hill School, Amery Hill

Why War?

Why war?
What's the point of blowing it up to its core?
Lives gone
This is all very wrong.

Why war?
Traumatic events
Making everyone feel tense
Do you have any sense?

Why war?
Unnecessary deaths
Everyone out of breath
Do you have a heart?

Why war?
Destroying everything in sight
Leaving nothing but spite
Is this helping?

Why war?
When the planet's gone
How are we going to live on?
Is peace ever an option?

Why war?
Trees and plants vanished

Everything banished
Why war?

Lauren Radley (14)
Amery Hill School, Amery Hill

Sadness...

You think you feel sadness,
Until you hit a spiral loop going down.

The world turns against you,
You're alone with nobody,
Thoughts fill your mind,
Overthinking every move; past, present and future,
You feel worthless,
To yourself and the world,
It's pain digging into you,
Going through your body,
Walking along a corridor of darkness,
With no light at the end.

It's an endless loop that comes to an end,
Different people,
Different times,
No matter how long it is,
There's always an end.

That's true sadness...

Eva Hunt (11)
Amery Hill School, Amery Hill

Rain

I hear the faint tip-tapping on her window,
I hear the rustle and bustle of people outside,
I see her leave her cosy confines,
But before she goes,
She opens her window and in the wind blows,
Dampening my translucent sheets.

I'm so cold.

I drift across her empty room,
Soon to be our empty tomb,
I gaze out her clean, clear window,
I see
Red,
Orange,
Then green.

I'm still cold.

I hear a loud crash,
Followed by loud, tortured wails,
But despite this...
I can still hear the faint tip-tapping on my window.

Rae Gershater (14)
Amery Hill School, Amery Hill

Change

Change can be good and change can be bad
Change can make people happy or sad
Like moving house or getting a new car
Like having fun at a new bar.

Change can make you feel happy and glad
Change can make you feel mad and sad
But climate change is bad
And you should not feel glad.

Climate change is horrible for our Earth
It's not a good future for the children we birth
It's not a good future for our Earth
It's not a good future for the people who surf.

So if we change our ways and do good
Then the world would be as it should.

Niamh Kennedy (12)
Amery Hill School, Amery Hill

Let's Take Action!

The planet we live on is a special place,
Populated by animals and the human race,
But now there comes a serious warning,
The newspapers teach us about global warming,
With temperatures increasing and sea levels rising,
Humans are in danger, it's hardly surprising,
Tons of plastic is polluting our seas,
The farmers' chemicals are hurting the bees,
Animals are dying, becoming extinct,
All of these problems seem to be linked,
The world fifty years ago was so much greener,
It is time to take action, let's help make the world cleaner.

Alice Barnett (11)
Amery Hill School, Amery Hill

Present To Future

The future beholds
Technology dependent thresholds
Embedded with innovation
Invented the power of teleportation
On other planets we have the ability to thrive
But still depending on oxygen to survive
To achieve this plastic must decay
Otherwise we may not live to see another day
For your children to experience this you must find it
In your heart to improve the climate
In the ocean, if islands of rubbish continue to form
Will you see your child's newborn
It's obvious what you need to do
How important is the Earth to you?

Sonny Taylor (14)
Amery Hill School, Amery Hill

Smiles!

Sometimes I feel like smiling,
Sometimes I don't at all.
A smile is more contagious than a frown,
So even if you are feeling down,
A simple smile will boost your mood,
It's also proven to be the most memorable feature of you!
Scientists have evidence to prove it reduces pain and stress,
Helping you live longer - isn't that the best?
Don't let any of the bad things get you down,
Be the positivity, not the letdown,
Every person deserves to express their happiness in style,
So do yourself a favour and embrace that smile!

Isabella Golding (11)

Amery Hill School, Amery Hill

Our Planet

Summer meadows
Swaying trees
Animals munching on the leaves
The man with the axe
Came to attack
The tree fell
Onto the floor
Too much fell
Almost too much to restore
That's not the only thing going on
The ice in the arctic is nearly gone
Due to the waste in the oceans
The amount is atrocious
Due to the fact of global warming
The world has been transforming
It's not looking good for our planet
But it's not too late to restore it
So come out and help me
Can anyone else agree?

Harry Wrout (11)
Amery Hill School, Amery Hill

The Birds Aren't Singing

The birds aren't singing.
Flying through the maze of towering trees,
Passing through the monkeys swinging
And the sloths sleeping in the warm breeze.

The birds aren't singing.
They can't sing whilst they fly through the trees,
They are crying.
All they fly over now is disgusting debris.

The birds are hiding.
The trees are on fire,
The rainforest is fighting.
Fighting against the humans' desire.

Now ruled by the king,
No longer can they sing.

Emily Mansbridge (14)
Amery Hill School, Amery Hill

Carefree

Why should I care about the future?
I will be dead.
So why should I care about my children?
I will be dead.
Stupid, dying polar bears
I'll be dead too.
Why should I be vegan?
I like the taste of meat.
The turtles would have died anyway
Why would they eat plastic?
Why should I care about the rainforests?
Let them burn down.
Let them burn fossil fuels
I want my electricity.
Kill the children
For all I care.
I'll be dead anyway
I'll be dead.

Harry Gibbs (14)
Amery Hill School, Amery Hill

A Balloon's Journey

Holding tightly, small fingers losing grip,
The balloon floats up, up and away,
Swaying smoothly, starting its trip,
The boy wants to follow, but gravity makes him stay.

Floating, floating above the trees,
Rising above the school,
Swaying softly in the breeze,
Above the clouds where the air is cool.

Flowing, flowing through heaven's gates,
The balloon reaches its resting place,
The angel's hands patiently wait,
A smile sits upon her face.

Belle Campion (11)

Amery Hill School, Amery Hill

Wonders Of The Winter Night

As the sun falls the moon rises,
The haunting hoot from the hunting owls fills the starry night,
Jack Frost puts on his dancing shoes and waltzes over car windows,
Leaving behind freezing, frosty footprints of iridescent swirls,
Snoozing squirrels and dozing dormice snuggle together, surrounded by their harvest hall,
As the warm glow from the street lamps flickers off, the sun begins to fill the sky with rosy pinks and wispy white clouds, with the promise of a crisp, new day.

Seren Chance (11)

Amery Hill School, Amery Hill

Environment

E veryone needs to save our world,

N umerous animals are dying,

V icious humans not caring for the world around us,

I believe we need to make a change,

R ainforests are being destroyed,

O ur world is dying,

N ature is being suffocated,

M istakes are slowly making our world crumble,

E very animal deserves to live,

N o one should live in a world full of litter,

T oday we make a change.

Eliza Davis (11)

Amery Hill School, Amery Hill

Future

The future, what is it?
Is the future powerful?
Is the future positive?
Will it be nuclear?
Will it be clean?
Will there be a future?

Will the future be negative?
Is the future dirty?
Who will be alive?
Will there be leaders?
Will there be people?
Will there be a future?

Is the future technological?
Is the future clever?
Is the future bright?
Will it be green?
Will it be kind?
Will there be a future?

Elliot Kelley
Amery Hill School, Amery Hill

Refrigerator

R efrigerators are cold,
E specially if there is a freezer in it.
F rom the fridge comes so much food,
R eheat leftovers,
I ce compartment, frosty.
G rated cheese, handy.
E nergy-rating poor, what a surprise.
R ed hot chili peppers.
A nts crawl in if you don't shut the door,
T rampling on your pristine butter
O r, you could shut the door on your
R efrigerator.

Ben Darroch (12)

Amery Hill School, Amery Hill

Boom

Boom.
By me, myself and I.

Tick.
Tick.
Tick.
Tick,
Tick,
Tick, tick, tick
Tick, tick, tick, tick, tick, tick, tick!

Why?

Why here?
Why now?
Why this poem?
In fact, why everything?

This poem has no answers.
I have no answers for you.
I only know one thing
And that is that the clock is
Ticking.
Tick.
Tick.

Boom.
By you, yourself and not just I.

Thomas Mossman (14)
Amery Hill School, Amery Hill

Environment

Petite turtles
Sapphire, cream waves and sand
Stepping, hatching into their eternal rest, not knowing what
could happen.

Waddling onto the transparent ice
Sliding, huddling all day long
Darkness fills them inside.

Stepping along the murky wilderness
Spring, delightful hedgehogs
But soon it all goes black.

Tigers prancing up and down
Creeping, threatening their prey
Crunching on their carcass that day.

Summer Wells (11)

Amery Hill School, Amery Hill

The Environment

Global warming,
Rain is pouring,
The planet's barely enduring.
Trees burning,
Chainsaws churning.
Animals hiding,
Poachers finding.

Ice caps melting,
Fuel smelting.
Hot summers, hosepipe bans,
Not enough water across the land.

What can we do to help now?
Anything might help to turn it around.
Let's bike to school and not take the car,
Use your feet if you're not going far.

Samuel Barlow (11)
Amery Hill School, Amery Hill

Whatever The Weather

Whatever the weather is,
Whether it's raining or snowing,
Sunny or foggy,
Or even all of the above.

Whether it's cloudy or stormy,
Drizzling or thundering,
Hailing or overcast,
Or even two at the same time.

Whether it's frosty or windy,
Full of tornadoes or hurricanes,
Raining with a bit of sunlight,
Or even a partly cloudy night.

I,
Will always be with you...

Daisy Scott-Gould (11)
Amery Hill School, Amery Hill

The Night Sky

S tars shimmer in the winter's night,
T winkling, dancing, speaking,
A quarius, Cancer, Pisces,
R iver of light that shines bright,
S teal the sky of darkness and make it light.

S hooting stars flying by,
H eaving, weaving, whizzing,
I ce belts, comets, meteors,
N ight-time's when you come alive,
E nticing us with your dive.

Evarni Brennan-Gott (11)
Amery Hill School, Amery Hill

Devices

"Watch where you're going,"
Said the crumpled old man with the stick.
Looking up from her phone and coming out of her zone,
She moves the pram around the man with the stick.
The tablet tumbles as fast as the baby's tears as it disappears,
"Look what you've done!"
The end has come.
Connection has stopped but the penny hasn't dropped,
Where do we go from here?

Finn Whittington (14)

Amery Hill School, Amery Hill

Life's Too Complicated

I think we need to go back to caveman times
Our society is too advanced
People might say we earned this luxury
Then we also earned a slow, horrible death by global
warming
When we were cavemen there wasn't much pollution
Now there is too much pollution
Cavemen were simpler people
The life of a caveman may have been harder
But nicer, no phones, no computers
No schools, no cars.

Cain Christmas (14)
Amery Hill School, Amery Hill

The Elements

Haiku poetry

Air
Unpredictable
Calm and pure, fresh and forceful
Free, no boundaries.

Fire
Blazing, burning flames
Forging a path of bright light
Wildfire spreads and sings.

Water
Koi carp dive in blue
Gem droplets dance like dragons
Crystal waters bright.

Earth
Mountains guard secrets
Ancient giants forged from stone
A haven for all.

Max Chesterman (11)
Amery Hill School, Amery Hill

Game Over

The games that have come before,
We can never restore,
'Cause every game ever,
Will not stay forever.

Overwatch, it had to stop,
It was good but not understood,
The queue to get in it was too long.

Fornite, you could not play,
Unless you play it at night,
So people did not see you,
Otherwise, there was nobody on to lead you.

Finley Cole (12)
Amery Hill School, Amery Hill

No Other Place Like Earth

E nvironment
N o other place like Earth
V iciously fighting for it
I t's dying!
R uining our world
O ur lovely world
N o other place like Earth
M any trees are gone
E very animal is fighting
N o other place like Earth, let's stop this and...
T reat our world kindly.

Maddy Keat (11)

Amery Hill School, Amery Hill

Why I Miss Spring

The warming sun awakes me,
The way the sun glistens above my face,
The wind gliding above the blooming flowers.
Trees remind me of a man,
Swaying in the wind,
Like the tree is saying hello.
A man with branches and leaves.
I run In the wInd,
Feeling the grass along my ankles.
The way the birds sing still rings in my ears.

Ellie Proud (11)
Amery Hill School, Amery Hill

Wild

The wild has hidden,
With forests in division
And the river that no longer flows.
Animals lay silent
Due to the violence
With nowhere else to go.
We attack and take,
Steal and fake,
Yet we still call them the foe?
The wild has hidden.
The world's in division.
It's finally time to say no.

Jake Stone (14)

Amery Hill School, Amery Hill

Our Planet

A nother day has gone by
N othing has changed
I deas are formed to stop this crime
M ammals, fish, reptiles, birds and amphibians have fallen to this crime
A nd we just stand there taking no stand on this matter
L ook towards this future of ours, these natural beasts won't be in it.

Luke Baldwin (13)
Amery Hill School, Amery Hill

Birdsong

A black bird always imagines
A yellow moon glowing
Through the dark sky.
But the clever owl remembers
The sad truth of old
Through a window of rain:
Does that mountain of gentle wondering
Pretend to walk and hide where joy is laughing?
No song whispers like a ghost in a dream
Or the chorus of an owl.

Florence Vickery (14)
Amery Hill School, Amery Hill

Sam The Bee

Buzzy bees, flying from flower to flower,
Buzzy bees, dodging big, hairy spiders,
Buzzy bees, making golden honey,
Buzzy bees, sleeping in their golden nest,
Buzzy bees, feed pollinated food for the family.

Six bees, sleeping tight until morning light,
Sleep tight in the night,
Buzzy bees...

Lexi-Grace Harrison (11)
Amery Hill School, Amery Hill

Creature

C reator of fear
R eigning terror through the night
E erily moving through the shadows
A formidable, repulsive sight
T errifying all other beings
U rban legend you are not
R elentless, deadly pursuit
E nding all who cross his path.

Max Bryant (11)

Amery Hill School, Amery Hill

Autumn

A uburn leaves twirling down from the large trees.
U mbrellas opening and closing.
T he sky fills with mist and crystal droplets.
U nderneath the grey clouds appears a natural world.
M agic flies through the air.
N ext autumn will come soon.

Gia Atayde (11)
Amery Hill School, Amery Hill

Autumn

Leaves dancing in the wind
A million colours of pure beauty
The crisp autumnal air will give you quite a freeze
The trees are no longer fruity
Dusk creeping in early
Sun rising later each day
The geese take on quite a journey
To the afternoon sun, where they lay.

Isla Pooley (12)

Amery Hill School, Amery Hill

Change

Trees chopped
Ice crumbles
Landfill burns
More waste tumbles.

Seas poisoned
Oceans not blue
Animals dying
Soon will you.

You live your life
Like any other day
You ignore the people
Who want to say
Save our planet!

Patrick Newman (11)
Amery Hill School, Amery Hill

Trees

Haiku poetry

Trees. Shift through the wind
How you creak and how you howl
Where have you gone to?

A noise... A thunder...
Rumble... Heavy machines
Crushing and crashing.

Destroying your home
What will you all do?
Nothing. You're a tree...

Oscar Welbourne (11)

Amery Hill School, Amery Hill

Barry B Benson - Save The Bees

I'm Barry B Benson,
Do I deserve all of this?
I pollinate your flowers so you can survive all of this;
But your smoke
Makes me choke
And we just can't understand
How you treat the only ones that give you hope
On a piece of hopeless land.

Emily Hagan-Corbridge (14)
Amery Hill School, Amery Hill

Think About The Bees

Did you know that...
Over one million bees die from pesticides a year?
Did you know that...
Bees help us grow kiwis and various other fruits each year?
Did you know that...
Bees will go extinct in the next hundred years?
So, think about the bees.

Fynn Eldridge (12)
Amery Hill School, Amery Hill

Is It Too Late?

Haiku poetry

The world needs saving
Science cannot help us now
There's no Planet B.

The crops are failing
The animals are starving
Cities are flooding.

The Earth needs our help
Can we learn from our mistakes?
We need to act now!

Lucas Fowell (11)
Amery Hill School, Amery Hill

The Tree Of Life

Haiku poetry

Twisted colours brown
A gorgeous spiral of wood
Reaching for the sky.

Cotton-soft so sweet
Gently swaying petals, pink
Blossoming with joy.

Nature's masterpiece
A warming sign of springtime
Cherry blossom tree.

Stanley Lloyd Pagett (11)

Amery Hill School, Amery Hill

Reminiscence

On this hill stands,
An ancient wood.
Watching over colourful lands,
And centuries stood.
Great branches outstretch,
And roots deep underground.
Two lovers' initials are etched,
To the tree's wrinkled bark It's bound.

Abigail Warburton (15)
Amery Hill School, Amery Hill

A Dog's Life

One pretty dog, lying in the sun
Golden fur, just like her mum
Licking and scratching, not a care in the world
Dozing and sleeping, all happy and curled
A dog's life it is, chilled and breezy
Oh, I wish my life was this easy.

Tom Abbott (11)

Amery Hill School, Amery Hill

Cheese

C heese is so yummy.
H ow many cheeses could I eat?
E ating cheese makes me feel funny.
E ven the best cheese smells like feet.
S o please just get in my tummy.
E very single cheese is so neat.

Tyler Oakley (11)
Amery Hill School, Amery Hill

Women, Life, Liberty

Protest chants for change,
Men and women stand as one,
For what they dream of.
Controlling Iran,
Morality police judge,
Women's rights matter.
Mahsa Amini,
Sacrificed her life for liberty,
Women will fight on!

Evie Ayres (11)
Amery Hill School, Amery Hill

All About Pups

P uppies will walk about,
U se a lead for their walks,
P uppies, puppies, they will cuddle with you,
P uppies, they snuggle with you when you're feeling lonely,
Y ou will love them with your heart.

Lilly Clarke (11)

Amery Hill School, Amery Hill

Food

Avocados chomped
Burgers get fried
Chicken sliced
Drinks are drunk
Eggs are poached
French fries are dipped
Gherkins are gross
Hash browns are hot
Ice creams are cold
Jed eats it all.

Jed Carter (14)

Amery Hill School, Amery Hill

Fish

Flipping, flopping in the sandy beach
Not able to breathe with plastic on them
Plastic, plastic, killing fish
Trapping them with a bottle or a bag
Eating pieces of plastic.

Finlay Peters-Kelly (11)
Amery Hill School, Amery Hill

Climate Change

Ice cap,
Polar, extensive,
Melting, slimming, deteriorating,
Factory, greenhouse gases, fumes,
Thawing, temperature rising,
Glistens, slippery,
Glacier.

Edmund Mellon Backhouse

Amery Hill School, Amery Hill

Arctic

A diamante poem

Arctic,
Vast, wild,
Freezing, roaming, trekking,
Polar bear, icebergs, explorer, footprints,
Hunting, discovering, resting,
Subzero, icy,
Glistening.

Ted Johnson (12)

Amery Hill School, Amery Hill

Dogs

A diamante poem

Dogs
Protective, tricked
Walking, fetching, fighting
Owners, puppies, sensitive, traumatised
Loving, bred, killed
Loveable, pieces
Abused.

Ruby Denman (11)

Amery Hill School, Amery Hill

Growing Alone

A diamante poem

Seed
Boring, dull
Crawling, struggling, climbing
Days, weeks, months, petal
Blossoming, developing, persevering
Alone, resilient
Flower.

Isabella (11)
Amery Hill School, Amery Hill

Oceans

A diamante poem

Oceans
Flowing, unloved
Listening, lurking, clashing
Coral, pollution, toxin, scorn
Tumultuous, evolving, vast
Calming, azure
Creatures.

Florence Marshall (11)

Amery Hill School, Amery Hill

Glaciers

A diamante poem

Glaciers
Frozen, towering
Melting, crying, disappearing
Ice, lagoon, sea, ocean
Rising, flowing, crashing
Torrential, endless
Water.

Denzel Cristian Cabaya Cerias (11)
Amery Hill School, Amery Hill

Life And Death

Life,
Beautiful, joyful,
Reuse, reduce, recycle,
Nature, Earth, plastic, litter,
Consume, destroy, stop,
Devastating, rapid,
Death.

Freya Twaite

Amery Hill School, Amery Hill

Fire And Ice

A diamante poem

Fire
Burning, boiling
Panicking, perishing, trembling
Smoke, heat, frozen, bitter
Fear, unsettling, worrying
Cruel, dangerous
Ice.

Isla Saunders (11)

Amery Hill School, Amery Hill

Fluid

A diamante poem

Lava
Heat, flaming
Melting, popping, burning
Volcano, fire, river, ocean
Reflecting, flowing, soaking
Peaceful, gentle
Water.

Aadi Patel (12)

Amery Hill School, Amery Hill

Polar Bear

Polar bear
Running, roaring
Sad, afraid, scared
Penguins, seals, plastic, rubbish
Worried, hated, alone
Crying, flying
Trash.

Archie Maloney (11)
Amery Hill School, Amery Hill

Sea

A diamante poem

Sea
Wavy, splashy
Swimming, living, dying
Fish, dolphins, jellyfish, sharks
Eating, cooking, selling
Blood, torture
Death.

Emily Carter (11)

Amery Hill School, Amery Hill

Ocean

A diamante poem

Ocean
Powerful, strong
Growing, splashing, crashing
Water, waves, sand, land
Shrinking, drowning, dying
Weak, weary
Land.

Jed Bentley (11)
Amery Hill School, Amery Hill

Polluted

Clean
Happy, joyful
Growing, forests, peaceful
New, life, dying, life
Forest, fires, threatening
Sad, miserable
Polluted.

Macey Bain (12)
Amery Hill School, Amery Hill

The Ocean

A diamante poem

Sea,
Pretty, blue,
Sky, moving, crashing,
Stones, windy, grass, shells,
Clouds, stopping, starting,
Light, dark,
Sand.

Destiny Rayne Cicley Bevan (12)

Amery Hill School, Amery Hill

Rabbits

A diamante poem

Rabbits
Small, fluffy
Bouncing, running, jumping
Bowl, toys, bed, lead
Sleeping, snoring, turning
Big, floppy
Bunnies.

Daisy Coulson (12)
Amery Hill School, Amery Hill

Environment

Environment
Recycling, saving
Enchanting, flourish, blooming
Planting, watering, reduce
Pollution, helping
Garden, flowers.

Trinh Tran (11)
Amery Hill School, Amery Hill

Pandas!

Pandas,
Hungry pandas,
Crying, wailing, sobbing,
Bamboo, trees, gone,
Let them have,
Wonderful, delicious,
Bamboo.

Lexie Ewart (11)

Amery Hill School, Amery Hill

Pets

A diamante poem

Pets
Lazy, quiet
Sleeping, grooming, hunting
Bed, food, sun, home
Playing, loving, exploring
Funny, relaxed
Cats.

Kayleigh Swinton (11)

Amery Hill School, Amery Hill

My Dog Called Lolli

Lolli
Kind, gentle
Eating, sleeping, barking
Ears, nose, eyes, tail
Lazy, walking, waddling
Old, slow
Lolli.

Jake Wray (11)
Amery Hill School, Amery Hill

Gaming

Gaming
Fun, easy
Relaxing, frustrating, levelling up
Win, lose, happy
Cool, nice
Game over.

Jack Harness (11)
Amery Hill School, Amery Hill

The Flying Wolf

A haiku

The grey wolf climbing,
Swiping for free food flying,
Feeding its six cubs.

Morgan-Jay Barrow (12)

Amery Hill School, Amery Hill

Sincerities

I'm sorry,
That we can't be friends,
That it's been over a year,
That nothing will change.

I'm sorry,
That I had 'too much emotion',
That I was 'so selfish',
That I was 'too boring'.

I'm thankful,
That you constantly knew how I felt,
That my memories are positive,
That you made me love myself.

I'm thankful,
That you were always there,
That you would stick up for me,
That there was so much we shared.

I wish,
That we had had more time,
That we still had contact,
That we could just share a smile.

I wish,
That maybe if I had been

A different person entirely,
We could still be we.

I wish,
Well I wish about a lot,
But most of all,
I wish you hadn't forgot.

Esmay Fairbairn (14)
Berwick Academy, Spittal

The Worrying War

Let our thoughts and prayers be with those in Ukraine,
As we think of all those people in pain.

The artillery and shells are coming down fast,
How long can this really last?

Russia is invading,
But they are slowly fading.

Ukraine are holding on tight,
As they fight with all their might.

When the soldiers leave they say 'goodnight'
As soon they will shine, like a ray of light.

Russia is invading,
But they are slowly fading.

By the trenches the soldiers hold their breath,
Waiting, waiting for their death.

Fighting for freedom, fighting for their home,
We will not let Russia take over and roam!

Russia is invading,
But they are slowly fading.

Romilly Oliver (14)
Berwick Academy, Spittal

Global Warning

Carbon emissions cloud the air,
Gradually producing the world's despair,
The sun's rays shine down around all,
With no interference, we'll cause our downfall,
With that being said - this is a warning,
We need to stop global warming.

Trees falling - stripped from the Earth,
We need to start our world's rebirth,
Sea levels rise as glaciers thaw,
Consequences that we foresaw,
Yet nothing happened - nothing changed,
Heating the Earth is what people maintained.

So I'll put it straight - before it's too late,
Let's fix the world to the best of our ability,
As it is our responsibility.

Joseph Todd (14)
Berwick Academy, Spittal

World War Two

W e held our hands to our heart,
O verlooking the ones who have played their final part,
R eady to take vengeance over the Germans,
L eading the line across the trenches,
D eath looking into our faces.

W e held our hands to our heart,
A ngry, we were finishing this war,
R eady to leave and see our family.

T ens of millions were dead,
W e held our hands to our heart,
O ver, the war was.

Alfie Wilson (15)
Berwick Academy, Spittal

Ruin

The water bill you cannot pay,
The bailiff's at the door, that you no longer can delay.

The empty kitchen cupboards lay bare,
The once common comforts, that now are rare.

The impossible debt you owe,
The fuel indicator on your car, that now reads 'low'.

Your 'living' wage is no longer liveable,
The polluted air is no longer breathable.

The town you grew up in, is now a ruin.

Craig Hiroz (14)

Berwick Academy, Spittal

Pollution Crisis

P lenty of pollution fills the environment.
O verfilled with plastic.
L eft to ruin the world we live in.
L ives of innocent animals taken.
U nder the risk of sea levels rising.
T urtles are stuck
I nside plastic bags and abandoned nets.
O ceans become filled with rubbish instead of sealife.
N ature reserves, ruined as factories take over.

Maddie Ferrell (14)
Berwick Academy, Spittal

Annihilation

A once vibrant green and lively home,
Quickly turned into a neglected planet,
Where only debris and litter could roam.

No signs of human life were in sight,
Only signs of decay and death,
Showing when humans had given up their fight.

Innocent creatures forced to flee,
Expanding factories, pollution and smog,
Cruelly destroying where their home used to be.

Isabella McPherson (14)
Berwick Academy, Spittal

A Joker's Jackpot

They laugh and they joke
They teased as she spoke
Not a kind word was spread
Her heart felt like lead
The school must've won the lottery
As she was now the class mockery.

Yet no one took notice
So they can taunt and provoke us
We will not remain quiet
No matter how much you deny it
You shattered her purities
And left behind many insecurities.

Ruby Haldon (14)
Berwick Academy, Spittal

My New Home

I swim to the school of fish,
My head bumps into something, wonder what it is?
I swim around bumping into every corner of this thing,
A bottle, that's what it is!
Dark, cold and scary around me,
I want to go home.
Plastic bags floating down towards the bottle I'm stuck in,
I want to go home.
The school moves into the distance,
I guess this is my new home.

Imogen Meakin (14)

Berwick Academy, Spittal

What Makes Men And Women Different?

A man can cry.
A man can vote and work.
A man can buy his second car for his garage.
But 'a man cannot cook, cannot stay at home and raise his kids', they say.
But 'a woman cannot fight, cannot stand up against a crowd and cannot speak', they say.
A woman can buy her second car for her garage.
A woman can vote and work.
A woman can cry.

Imogen Mitchell (14)
Berwick Academy, Spittal

Anonymous

Lack of trust from a country,
To one of which neighbours Hungary.
Russia and Ukraine will never be the same,
With bombs going off every day.

With prices of essentials going up,
It's just like a bad break-up.
With people low on money and businesses closing,
It's just like the whole world is decomposing.

Emily Parsons (14)
Berwick Academy, Spittal

Occupation

Nowhere to go, no way out,
Fighting for freedom,
Freedom from constant changes,
A constant battle,
Every time you win, you lose twice,
Deeper and deeper,
More pressure, more pain,
Drowning in a pit of despair,
Endlessly deep, no way out,
The endless, constant battle for freedom.

William Gilchrist (14)
Berwick Academy, Spittal

Patriarchy

The climb to the top is tough
But the top isn't enough
Women working while
Men make the most money.
Women expected to stay home and waste their potential
While men work all day with more praise
Patriarchy runs the people
Patriarchy runs the world.

Heidi Scott (14)

Berwick Academy, Spittal

The Declining State Of Earth

Fire and flood
The world's gone mad
Millions are suffering
Millions are dying
So many, too many are desperately sad
The Earth is sighing
The Earth is crying
Will somebody please help?

Stuart Wakenshaw (14)
Berwick Academy, Spittal

To My Dear...

To my dear,

As I write this,
The crisp pearly snow gently sprinkles upon us,
Swiftly sharing its icy breath with the surroundings.
Just like the chilly morning we met,
I'd never forget.
Meeting you made me feel alive once again,
For the last time.

Your mellow voice that caressed my ears,
The thought of having your dainty porcelain fingers
betrothed to me,
Or that sparkling smile that shone brighter than the stars,
Those were the things that made my innocent heart beat
out of my chest.

I'm sorry for not telling you earlier,
I would have never thought we would be parting ways.
I'm going to die soon,
However I'll leave without regrets.
That's what I'd like to confidently say,
The honest truth is,
I have one,
And it's that I never got the chance to marry you.

From your everlasting love.

Sumedha Suntharalingam (15)
Brentside High School, Ealing

Dear Mum

I was never enough

I looked into your mesmerising blue eyes,
And I knew you were my home.
But you looked at me with eyes of spite.
Since then, I knew, I was never enough.

Dad left me, he never came back,
You spent nights crying on the cold floor,
Waiting for him to come back.
When he didn't, you blamed it on me
But I didn't care,
Instead all I did was agree.

You told me of your old life,
How dazzling, eccentric and playful it was,
You then told me how I cut you away from it like a knife.
Taking all the pleasure you had away from you.

You told me about how you would go out with your friends
every night,
I would listen to you, imagining your excitement,
But then you would look at me like I was blight,
Saying how it was all my fault, you could never do it again
Since then, I knew, I was never enough.

I went to high school,
I didn't fit in well there,

I tried to be cool
But they didn't want me either.

I told you about it,
I complained, I cried
You listened but then you said it would have never
happened if I was fit.
But that didn't matter, because you only did it because you
cared.

I started struggling with my grades,
It wasn't my fault, it was hard for me to understand,
But you were there and you explained everything through
charades.
And I saw how you really did care.

But then I asked, how you were so good,
And you complained how I took you away from the game
you loved most,
So I turned around, to cover my tears, with my hood.
Hoping you never saw.

This Mother's Day, Mum,
I would like to return everything to you,
Your old life, your hobbies and even your favourite
bubblegum.

I will not be able to return the 13 years I stole from you,
But I hope you can get them back,
And finally enjoy that job you looked so forward to.

I love you, Mum, no matter what,
You were always my idol, my hope and my joy,
I hope one day we meet again, but
This time in Heaven where you will come not to complain,
But to hug me and kiss me, the same way I did to you.

Fatimah Shah (15)
Brentside High School, Ealing

It's Not Just Us Here

Animals, they are all around,
Big or small, green or brown
However, an obstacle has occurred,
So this is the time to spread the word.
Those precious souls are being endangered,
We must join together, friends or strangers!
Charities, they are all around,
They save animals from going down.
Just by donating, you can help save many,
Any donation helps them, light or heavy.
So tell me, are you ready to save some?
And let our animals experience real fun!
The good thing is you don't have to give money,
Any donation is great, from clothes to honey!
So tell me, are you ready to aid?
Aid our animals through this barricade!
So tell me, are you ready to assist?
Without your help, they surely will be missed!
So tell me, are you ready to help animals on sea or
underground?
Because animals, they are all around.

Mischa Nicolas (13)

Brentside High School, Ealing

Normal School Day

It's like any other day,
I pack my bag, I go to school
With my food and pride.
I guess I take myself for a fool
That's when it happens
All hell breaks loose.

I run like there's no tomorrow
Praying to God I hope it's not true
This was the effect of Operation Blue Star.
I see my mum lying on the floor
Telling me not to open the door
She tells me not to come close
I guess I knew her the most.
I didn't.
I feel my body weaken,
Like it's shedding to the floor.
She tells me to go and I try to say no
But I knew she won't
I guess I knew her the most
I go outside and all I see are familiar faces,
Faces that I have seen around.
To my surprise I find blood.
It rushes to my head,
No one to call out to
Or I'll be dead.

I move as fast as possible
Yet all I see is the sky
I don't want to die
To my surprise I taste blood.

Krishmit Singh (14)
Brentside High School, Ealing

Happier Days

Every day, on the news, we hear something bad, worse
than the day before.
About gang crime, suicide, civil wars and more.
About environmental issues, kidnapping, child labour galore.
Children scared, parents depressed, starvation, the list
goes on.
But when is enough, enough?
When will we focus on the good?
Young children following their dreams, contributing to
saving our planet, spending time with loved ones.
Don't you want that?
Don't we all?
When I walk out on the street, I want to feel safe, happy.
"Oh forget it, it doesn't matter!"
I've heard it all before.
So it's time we stand together, and put a stop to it all.
Smile at strangers, help me, help you.
Try to be nicer, kinder, happier.
Try your best to smile.
It will all work out, in a little while!

Sharae Hay (12)
Brentside High School, Ealing

Let's Make A Change

U ncountable tragedies and Ukraine is trying, trying to
fight Putin's backseat driving. All of the news stories,
have all said, "It will get better," while in

K yiv, everyone has had a drafting letter. Everything

R ight now is being destroyed, every single soldier is being
deployed.

A ll anyone is thinking is, *when will this be over?* We really
need some luck right now, a four-leaf clover. We
searched all over just to gain some

I ntel, but we've given up now, our morale has fallen.

"N ever give up," they say. "Stand for Ukraine." Even if it's a
struggle or a big pain.

E veryone has shown their respect but it's time for action,
otherwise what can you expect? Another month,
another year? That is not okay, stop sitting back, let's
make a change!

Myles Cayford (13)

Brentside High School, Ealing

Home

This is not a book of life, but a story.
When we wake up and get out of bed,
You sit down, watching the news, scratching your head.
It's there, it's everywhere.
They sit on the floor, on the streets,
Looking for some comfort and warmth.
It's them, they need a home,
They need some food and drink.
They need to be comfortable in their own skin.
The cost of living, rising up and up.
Rising like a balloon filled with helium,
Which was let go by an unfortunate child.
It could get stuck or just rise
Until, it pops and the price of living is lowered.
They are like sitting ducks.
They sit and sit and then, *bang!*
One thing is for sure, that one day, one day,
I hope, I desperately hope that someone
With a good soul and big heart
Will change the world.

Udaya Thapa (12)
Brentside High School, Ealing

School's Too Long

School is too long, it's like a prison.
Forced in to work and ruining our sleep.
Adults say we need to go to school.
Yes, we do but not 30 hours a week.
Why can't it be 9:30 to 3:00?
Five days a week is too long,
However, four days is just right.
School ruins teens' sleep schedule
Because we sleep late
And have to wake up early
And all the homework is insane!
We can get six pieces every single week.
The complicated rules are mad,
One minute late equals a thirty-minute after-school
detention.
You can be in all classes without your friend
On the other side of the room.
That just makes school boring
And unenjoyable for you to learn.

Rudin Nika (13)
Brentside High School, Ealing

Be Happy Instead Of Not Being Happy

Why would you be depressed when you can be happy?
If you're happy the world will be a better place
Gloomy people make others feel unhappy
The world will be brighter if you're happy.

Why would you be depressed when you can be happy?
Everything is much more fun when you are joyful
School was more fun for me.
I feel more confident now.

Why would you be depressed when you can be happy?
Your negativity takes you nowhere but bad outcomes
Positivity takes you to good outcomes.

So, why would you be depressed when you can be happy?
You should be happy.

Mariya Kimura (13)
Brentside High School, Ealing

Stop Cyberbullying

Bullying has caused so much damage over the years.
It has caused depression and even suicide.
To bully is to show cowardice.
A bully puts others down, usually with their words and
actions, judging them.
Sadly, this only reveals who the bully is...
A person who puts others down to feel better about
themselves.
Bullying can destroy a person emotionally.
It is foolish and dangerous.
If you are a victim of bullying, don't keep it a secret.
Get help.
You deserve to know just how many people have been in
your situation and are on your side of the battle.

Elifnur Soysal (11)
Brentside High School, Ealing

Two Genders

We live in a world filled with hate
Apparently,
Where this planet,
Believe men are stronger than women.

Attention attacks our minds
Like money
And other greedy things.

Our world sees mighty men as kings,
What about our women?
If men lead like lions,
Why are women
Only seen as mice?

Why do women
Always feel scorn around men?
Why do men
Always feel like kings around women?

Most women have been hiding
From the utopia they desire.
Most women have never touched this luxury.

Eloise Nateguy (11)
Brentside High School, Ealing

Winter

The hot weather starts to fade away
And bitter cold nights are creeping in,
When people get home they grab their blankets
And the hot chocolate tin.
People start thinking of activities
Like ice-skating or movie nights,
I have heard that people are already on Amazon
Buying a lot of Christmas lights.
All the decorations for Halloween
Are being taken down rapidly,
For the gigantic Christmas theme.
Everyone is out buying presents
For the best winter birthdays,
Outside there is snow
And mistletoe, in all the doorways.

Maia Alves Da Silva (13)
Brentside High School, Ealing

Our Planet

We only have one planet
Our Earth is dying
And there's no cure.

We are damaging, polluting and destroying our Earth.
Can you not see the trees dying
And the sea drying!
Along with the deadly smog disguised as pollution
The animals that have succumbed to their death because of plastic.
In addition to the humans who are too selfish to recycle.
We need to be aware of the conflict we are creating.

The Earth is slipping away
And it's up to us to make sure it stays.

Yasmin Gelle (13)
Brentside High School, Ealing

The Mask

One day the world looked into her eyes
They said it is as low as the sun setting before a summer's night
Her smile
Do I dare to say
It was as bright as the sun rising in July
But who knew how much she hid inside.

Her mask was wearing off
Cracks that left a shadow
That were once used to illuminate light.
The paint that once covered her scars is now running down
Running down as it holds onto a lifeline
She said, "Is this how it feels to be eaten alive?"

Olla Shawari (13)
Brentside High School, Ealing

Everyone Deserves...

We need your attention...

People are getting bullied every day for just who they are or can't do what they want to do without being judged.
Everyone deserves to have an education.
Everyone deserves to have a job.
Everyone deserves to have shelter.
Everyone deserves to have food and water.
It doesn't matter if you're black, white, Muslim, Buddhist, straight, trans...
Everyone deserves to be respected.
Everyone deserves to have basic human rights no matter what.

Zahraa Ataya (11)
Brentside High School, Ealing

Another Year

Another year,
Another tear.
Another day of sadness,
Another day of madness.

It's not fixed,
Why can't girls do what boys can?
Why can no one speak up?

Another year,
Another tear.
Another day of sexism,
Another day of racism.

It's not fixed,
We have rights.
A right to live.
We all need to support equality.

A new year,
A new tear.
A new way to start,
A new way to end.

Ema Subert-Shikama (11)
Brentside High School, Ealing

Truth Of The World

It's not the place we called peaceful and calm
It's not the place we thought was safe
It was all just a bunch of lies
It's the place we'd be in danger anytime.

It's the place where death is common all the time
The world we thought was equal
The world we thought was safe
It was all hidden.

Hidden down below until discovered
That's the truth of the world
People need to know
One way or another.

Neameh Al-Talha (11)
Brentside High School, Ealing

Deforestation

The remaining forest...
Cutting down trees and lovely branches.
Forests satisfy us,
We admire all the lovely nature and surroundings,
Walking down the lovely forest
With our friends, and families
And walks with our dogs.

Thinking soon it will all be cleared for human activities.
Making space for humans to use.
Lovely wood used for logs to set up fires during winter days.

Safiya Noor (11)
Brentside High School, Ealing

Deforestation

Around the world, in the woods
Trees are apparently being cut down for good.

Around the world, around a factory
They use these poor animals' homes to make money.

In the wood, around the trees,
You see these callous humans doing this destruction for a bit of money.

Around the woods, around the trees,
You see squirrels struggling to supply food for their families.

Daniel Malaeb (11)
Brentside High School, Ealing

Why And What Have We Done To Deserve Such Life-Impacting Things?

Why, just why?

B ullying needs to stop
yo **U** can help stop bullying
L ife is not easy
L ife is like a dream but worse
Y ou can do something to stop bullying
I f you think positive it will come true
N othing is better than having a good life
G irls and boys, it is still a big problem, very big.

Gurleen Kour (11)
Brentside High School, Ealing

Racism

As I was walking down the street
An horrific sight made me stop my feet.
What I saw made me fall to the deck
A white man on a black man's neck.
Stopping him from breathing until he passed out.
My burning question is, why do people do this to others?
Cause discrimination and segregation when they should be
brothers.

Troy Mercan (11)
Brentside High School, Ealing

World Problems

From discrimination to child labour to bullying,
These are all problems we need to solve.
We need to solve them before our world dissolves.
Help us fight for the sake of the future
And rid the world of evil.
Because it's not one person's voice that matters,
It's everyone's.

Zayn Ali (11)
Brentside High School, Ealing

Labour Of Children

Children are just young citizens,
But children are hurt, burnt, dreaming and screaming,
All because of labour,
They don't get their voices heard,
They're in the scorching sun,
In the flooding rain,
In terrible pain,
Is this the life they're supposed to be in?

Armstrong Sutharsan (11)
Brentside High School, Ealing

Gangs

We all know 'em,
They beat
They steal
They shank
It's just terrible
So if we stand up
Secure our homes
I think we will be alright.

Redouane Boutiche (11)

Brentside High School, Ealing

A One-Way Trip

I come from a foreign land,
far away, where the bad guys once lived.
You shouldn't be scared, I'm not like them,
I am kind and playful,
the one you might like.
I come from the night sky on a rocky hill,
it is nice and bright, but we were not there for long.
The night sky of Berlin disappeared to bright lights in a
plane.
You know, I come from a place that was at war,
I will not speak of that man, a man who ruled.
Our ancestors will be proud.
I come from the dawn of sunlight near a large river,
you will know it, you probably know it,
a Mersey of the river.
I live near a grassy field where we play,
you might make some friends, who knows?
I may be there.
I come from an ancient ape who evolved into our ancestors
who once ruled the Earth,
without any cows,
this was our first evolution.

Robert Bollans (12)
Co-Op Academy Bebington, Wirral

All About Me

My name is Maisie, just like daisy,
I have two sisters and one brother,
I have a cat who is still a young age,
I have a PlayStation that I play on,
I have an amazing friend group and friends,
I have a Segway that I kinda play on,
I go to Bebington High School,
I had black hair when I was a baby but now I'm older, it went blonde,
My hair turns dark at winter times,
I have an amazing English teacher,
I have an amazing stepsister,
My cat is black and white,
I used to have a Samsung but I have an iPhone,
When I get home from school, I go on Snapchat and call my mates,
I give my cat three treats every day when I come home from school.

Maisie-Lea Allinson (12)
Co-Op Academy Bebington, Wirral

Waiting For Winter

The snowflakes fall as there's more snow,
The winter breeze is like a freezer,
The snow makes us make snow angels,
The snow is as soft as a feather,
Snowfields are just like a winter wonderland,
The fire glows as it heats us,
As Christmas comes by, the joy of people grows,
The winter clothes are just too soft and warm for summer,
As the night goes, bright lights shine,
You can see people with joy, with family inside,
The laughter of them makes my night glow,
So many houses are creative with the act of Christmas,
The presents are just as joyful as spending time with family.

Amelia Frost (12)
Co-Op Academy Bebington, Wirral

Siblings

It's me, just me now,
No more loud, bouncy airwaves,
No more being irritating,
No more being little,
Because he isn't here anymore.
He's gone, he left.
It's just me, me now,
Alone,
It was fun,
It was loud,
It was the usual life,
Until, until
He packed up and moved away.
Far away.
He's starting a new adventure,
Just one without me.
It's loud for him,
But quiet for me,
He's all grown up,
He's chosen his life,
And now it's time
To choose mine.

Amy Guttenberg (12)
Co-Op Academy Bebington, Wirral

My Life

I come from Birkenhead,
I have lived there for five years,
And it is a wonderful place to call home.

I come from Doctor Who,
It is my favourite TV show,
I love the Daleks and the 11th Doctor.

I come from Star Wars,
I love Darth Vader,
I prefer the Dark side.

I come from a big and busy school,
You may have heard of it,
The name starts with 'co-operative'.

I come from Harry Potter,
I love Voldemort,
My favourite film or book is The Deathly Hallows.

Kai Carress (12)
Co-Op Academy Bebington, Wirral

Fez

I come from a place called Rock Ferry,
I come from a place where the love of football is heavy,
I come from a place where we all carry knives,
I come from a place where a lot of people die,
I come from a place where we all wear ballys,
I come from a place where we aren't very fancy.

I come from a place where we all care,
I come from a place where we all share,
I come from a place where you're all welcome, no matter
where you are from.

Adam Fletcher (12)
Co-Op Academy Bebington, Wirral

I Come From

I come from the paint on the canvas of art,
My emotions are like messed up drawing and torn paper.
I come from a place where tech makes me happy
And coding is like making a custom character.
I come from Rock Ferry, a place people say we're like snails,
I live next to a park and Primary called Rock Ferry Primary School.
I have a variety of foods I like: pizza, popcorn,
Cheeseburgers, chips, chicken nuggets, chicken wings, and cheese and ham toasties.

Blake Pinch (12)
Co-Op Academy Bebington, Wirral

Same Old Rock Ferry

I come from a place where the younger generation is seen
as the downfall,
I come from a place where stabbings and robberies don't
even make the local Echo,
I come from a place where, if I walk down the road, people
shrink away in fear,
I come from a toxic area, where everyone is someone's
greatest hater,
Bright stars, dancers, boxers, footballers, singers, but no
opportunities,
I come from Rock Ferry, a place with no attention, no hope,
and no change.

Jake Devaney (12)
Co-Op Academy Bebington, Wirral

Who I Am

My name is Jacob,
Not everyone has my name,
Those who do are still not like me.

I like Splatoon 3,
See, not everyone is like me.

Those who like it are still not like me,
I like the Splat Dualies,
Are you still like me?

If you are, what's your last name?
Mine is Williams,
Jacob Williams, that is me.

This is who I am,
It's not just that,
There is much more to who I am.

Jacob Williams (12)
Co-Op Academy Bebington, Wirral

Life

I am a boy from Rock Ferry,
Where kids carry knives, committed to being a show-off,
Children run from the police,
Crimes every day.
A place where kids appear on Wirral Crimewatch,
Youngers taking drugs,
Minors stealing.
Yet I'm also from a place where the community helps the kids
By opening parks, and new equipment for parks,
A place where everyone is kind,
A place where you're not scared to walk outside.

Brodie Humphreys (12)
Co-Op Academy Bebington, Wirral

The Nordic

I come from the fjords, watching the view
and watching the mountain, towns, cities, and the
Norwegian sea.
I come from a city
where the city glows in the dark.
I come from a warm place,
where the sun makes everyone happy in the summer.
I come from a country
that has the most oil reserves in Europe.
I come from Norway,
a country that has beautiful fjords.
I play with Vikings.

Zaniar Baktiar (12)
Co-Op Academy Bebington, Wirral

The UK

I come from a place where football is life,
Where people aren't afraid to carry a knife,
These types of people may steal your bike.

The homeless beg for food and change,
Watching as the rich walk into The Range.

This country is corrupt,
The population about to erupt,
The rich get richer,
The poor get poorer.

Energy bills soar,
And always, war.

Toby Mccoy (12)
Co-Op Academy Bebington, Wirral

People, People Whistle By

People, people whistle by,
Whistle by,
Whistle by,
Some have coffee,
Some have tea.

People, people whistle by,
Whistle by,
Whistle by,
Some are black,
And some are white.

People, people whistle by,
Whistle by,
Whistle by,
Some have dogs,
Some have cats.

Though people, people whistle by,
Whistle by the same.

Aaron Minshull (12)
Co-Op Academy Bebington, Wirral

I Am From

I come from a place where people carry weapons,
And teenage boys roam the streets.
I come from a place where kids vape
And take drugs,
I come from a place where angry mobs stampede the
streets,
But
I come from a place where people work as a community,
I come from a place that has a great king,
I come from a place where all people are treated with
respect.

Jayden Davies (12)
Co-Op Academy Bebington, Wirral

Me

I am from Birkenhead,
Where people carry weapons,
Where people run from police,
Not always with something to hide.

Homeless people wander,
Begging for change,
While gangs loiter menacingly
Outside shops and streets.

But I also come from a place where
Footballs strike,
Kids play
And friendships last.

Alfie Westmoreland-Rigg (12)
Co-Op Academy Bebington, Wirral

My Life

L iverpool are my favourite team
U nlike Everton, who suck
K ernkraft 400 is a great song
E minem is a boring bomb

M o Salah is an Egyptian king
O degaard is a rubbish king
R uby, my fish, died
A DHD won't stop me
N atalie won't stop supporting me - my mum.

Luke Moran (13)

Co-Op Academy Bebington, Wirral

My Home

I'm from big football derbys,
Black bikes and knives all around,
Balaclavas and young thugs,
I come from an unknown town,
Outsiders know nothing about.

I'm from many new buildings,
Endless history and beaches,
I come from Rock Ferry,
A place of community,
A place of happiness,
A place of warmth.

Blake Boardman (12)
Co-Op Academy Bebington, Wirral

Living In Rock Ferry

I am from Rock Ferry,
Where people carry knives,
And where you get stereotyped.

I'm meeting my mates, not waiting for drugs,
I'm going out, not wanting trouble,
I'm not wanting to be stabbed.

You get the people in alleys,
Who come out in ballys,
They're the people you need to watch out for.

Adam Call (12)
Co-Op Academy Bebington, Wirral

My Community

I come from a place where people carry knives,
Where gangs run the night,
Where homeless people beg,
And screams fill the night.

I come from a place where the community is strong and loyal,
How would you feel?
You should feel good to be in such a loving community,
With lovely shopping centres and stunning rivers.

Luke Mansell (12)
Co-Op Academy Bebington, Wirral

I Come From

I come from the Blakeborough,
the best family,
made from food and emotion.

I come from fighting sports and clubs,
of the emotions
that are weak but hard to break.

I come from the Wirral,
a place of magic.
We have everything you can think of,
it's like Mary Poppins' bag,
but better.

Joey Blakeborough (12)
Co-Op Academy Bebington, Wirral

Home

I come from a place
Where happiness is aplenty,
I come from a place
Where violence is empty.

If you visit it,
You won't know what lonely is,
Unless you visit it,
You won't know how homely it is.

This place is what people call Bangalore,
This place is where I call home.

Havish Susanta Panda (12)
Co-Op Academy Bebington, Wirral

Ferry 'Til I Die

I come from the Ferry,
Where it is not that merry,
But besides the Rovers,
There is nothing to do,
Birkenhead is not the place to go,
With knives and sirens and roadmen with ballys,
Over the river from Liverpool,
There are no rules,
Except mopeds zooming past,
We have snobs eat Hobnobs.

Harvey Wright (12)
Co-Op Academy Bebington, Wirral

The Survival

I come from a place where people carry knives,
I come from a place where people wear ballys and ride bikes,
I come from a place where The Echo is found in most shops,
But I also come from a place where
You can have a laugh with your mates at any time,
Whether you're happy or sad,
The Wirral.

Alex O'Hanlon (12)
Co-Op Academy Bebington, Wirral

I Come From

I come home from school
and walk through the field with my friends every day,
I come from FIFA16, this is where my FIFA career began,
turning on my PlayStation every day.
I come from the Wirral, that's where I live,
with a family of four, I have a dog called Max,
and that's all.

Oliver Johnson (12)
Co-Op Academy Bebington, Wirral

I Come From

I come from music,
Of the weighted strings,
By the songs they create,
I come from the secret-keeping mask that lies on my face,
I come from those around me,
They built me and my heart,
I come from football and the influences of it,
I follow home,
And home is where family is.

Ryan Smith (12)
Co-Op Academy Bebington, Wirral

I Come From

I come from a place where teenagers travel in gangs,
Where people cross the road to avoid them,
Where everyone avoids alleyways.

I come from a place where the neighbours are friends,
And the kids get along well,
Where the parents are supportive,
And the community is strong.

Leighton Burke (12)
Co-Op Academy Bebington, Wirral

The Fez

I come from the Fez,
The streets are filled with hooligans,
Pigs chasing kids.

I come from the wastelands,
Strange people in every house,
Crimes every day.

I come from Rock Ferry,
Kids carrying knives,
Lads taking drugs,
People fighting over nothing.

Oliver Griffiths (12)
Co-Op Academy Bebington, Wirral

164

I Come From

I come from the Emirates Stadium,
the goals and assists by the people who play.
I come from the park after a late night playing football,
the fun and the memories are what matter.
I come from the PS4 after a long night with my mates,
the joy and the wins, it's like a pot of tens.

Austen Pedersen (12)
Co-Op Academy Bebington, Wirral

Where I Come From

I come from Tranmere,
Where the Rovers play,
Come rain or shine,
Here they stay.

I come from the football,
Where I follow Liverpool
On their road to glory.

But I also come from a place
Where gangs with knives
Rule and terrorise.

Lewis Knott (12)
Co-Op Academy Bebington, Wirral

I Come From Port Sunlight

I come from Port Sunlight,
A place with kindness and joy,
A place where you feel safe wherever you go,
Some people are cheerful,
Some are peaceful,
This is a lovely place for everyone,
There are many things to do,
There's always something for you.

Arron Mitchell (12)

Co-Op Academy Bebington, Wirral

He Comes And Goes

He comes from a place where animals live
until they are bought.
He comes to a place with a family
and is given the name of Ace.
He stayed in a cage
which he called home for life.
Until he goes to heaven,
after a long, happy life.

Archie Carrigan (12)
Co-Op Academy Bebington, Wirral

Lifestyle

I come from the wilderness of the outdoors,
I come from New Ferry, of the houses of the people years ago,
I come from Liverpool to do kickboxing,
I come from the food that the people enjoy,
The music that I enjoy comes from the people!

Bryn Essam (12)

Co-Op Academy Bebington, Wirral

William

W illiam is my name
I support Liverpool FC
L ove playing dodgeball
L ove playing football
I go to the park
A pples are my favourite fruit
M atch of the Day is my favourite TV show.

William Scott
Co-Op Academy Bebington, Wirral

I Come From

I come from London,
a place of the crown,
down in the south.

I come from McDonald's,
a place where there is food,
a place of joy.

I come from a good family,
a family of joy,
and a home of love.

Wentworth Smith (12)
Co-Op Academy Bebington, Wirral

My Life

I come from playing in the park with my mates,
I come from Rock Ferry, it is nice, dirty, and has a lot of good parks,
I come from playing on my Switch, I also play the Pokémon games,
I come from Bebington High School.

Taylor Anderton (12)
Co-Op Academy Bebington, Wirral

In The Night

Sirens blare,
Planes take flight,
Bombs are dropped in the night,
Explosives blow,
Soldiers fight,
People die, all in fright,
Engines roar,
Civilians hide,
Homes are destroyed, exploding in lights.

Joel-Peter Maddocks (12)
Co-Op Academy Bebington, Wirral

I Come From

I come from Rock Ferry,
from piles of cans.
I come from hours of gameplay on Steam,
from a family night of Dad winning board games.
I come from a family,
with a smile that gleams.

Taylor Lewis (12)
Co-Op Academy Bebington, Wirral

The Beautiful Game

I come from football,
that is what made me who I am.
I come from the beautiful game
filled with mixed emotions.
I come from football,
trying to be like one of my heroic heroes.

Jack Graham (12)
Co-Op Academy Bebington, Wirral

I Come From

I come from late nights on PC with friends,
I come from the Wirral,
I come from football matches in the park,
I come from Co-Op Bebington, on the way home,
I come from my mum.

Jack Johnson (12)
Co-Op Academy Bebington, Wirral

All About Me

My name is Owen,
Football is my game,
When I miss, I feel ashamed,
But when I score, I hear the crowd roar,
And when I get tackled, I get rattled.

Owen Harvey (12)
Co-Op Academy Bebington, Wirral

Me

F unny I am
I ntelligent I am
N ice I am
L aughing I like
E verton are bad
Y es, I am creative.

Finley Edge (12)
Co-Op Academy Bebington, Wirral

In My Eyes

When I see the man who cleans,
huffing and mumbling about grungy teens,
I feel like life ain't that bad,
he lives carefree and is allowed to be mad.
When I see the woman who cares,
talking sweetly to the sick,
I feel like life ain't so mean,
she's kind to all and can keep herself clean.
When I see the ones who yell,
preaching and damning wrong'uns to Hell,
I feel like life ain't absolute,
they were once scholars who settle a dispute.
When I see a stranger on the street,
going about their day and stopping for a greet,
I gain hope once again,
hope we can rinse out this bloodstain.
Bloodstains of the past haunt our lives,
our parents, our siblings, husbands and wives.
But by inspiring each other, we can change,
we can realise that life isn't so strange.
That is why I find inspiration outside,
in stranger's smiles and kind eyes.
Even if they wanna watch the world burn,
in everyone there is something we can all learn.

Ilianna Cartwright (15)
North Cambridge Academy, Kings Hedges

Heroes And Villains

Villains aren't born evil,
They become evil
Because they are mistreated
And humiliated
During their lives.
Sometimes, it's impossible to tell someone's
A villain, until it's
Too late.

But the difference
Between what we call
Villains,
And what we call
Heroes;
It's villains who would sacrifice
The world
For you,
While heroes
Would sacrifice
You
For the world.

This shows,
No one bad is every truly bad
And no one good is ever truly good,
They are seen as the storyteller sees them,

Monsters are made,
Not born.
Any soul tortured, confused insistently
Will have no time to mourn.
Remember, they too were once
Broken and frail.

So remember,
People change
For two main reasons:
Their minds have opened,
Or their hearts
Have been broken.

Ella Fordham (13)
North Cambridge Academy, Kings Hedges

Last Week's News

People are forgetting
because it's last week's news but
we
shouldn't, we mustn't, we
can't,
can't
forget
the horrors in Ukraine,
the struggle
and
pain of the families leaving soldiers behind,
life destroyed
in the cruel face of war; people
can't
feel safe anymore,
because their home is now a warzone.
If they possibly can, they
move,
because leaving is the only option left.
They are
on
a path scarier than
we
will ever
need

to know, so
to
everyone in the UK,
act
now,
help Ukraine.

Emma Thomas (13)
North Cambridge Academy, Kings Hedges

Blinding Inferno

Have you seen the fire, an orange light?
It's burning to a max, what a horrific sight!
But it's not just one fire, it's burning many hues,
The forest, the oceans, so many pressing issues.
You'll think it's fine, just carry on,
You've got to fight the problem, fight, be strong!
Because the ice is melting, there's way too few trees,
Can't you see it? Look harder, look for the catastrophes!
You'll carry on flying and driving, like nothing's happening,
Then beware, you will trigger things.

Alvar Meyer zu Eissen (12)
North Cambridge Academy, Kings Hedges

The Earth Is Dying

The Earth is dying
And everyone knows.
The Earth is dying,
With all its beauty.
The Earth is dying
And no one is helping.
The Earth is dying,
It's a gas tank.
The Earth is dying
Because of all the humans here.
The Earth is dying,
It was alive before,
Before all the humans,
Before all the factories, houses and wars.
The Earth is dying,
After every new car, every new piece of clothing.
The Earth is dying.
The Earth is crying.
The Earth is dead.

Ruth Dawson (12)
North Cambridge Academy, Kings Hedges

Greed

Humans and greed go together,
Between the oil and the coal,
The Earth will pay the ultimate toll.
Global warming, they call it,
I say it's the Earth's way
Of making us pay for the greed,
Ushering in natural disasters, which in turn
Threaten the human race as we know it.
Human greed will be our demise,
The key to saving Earth is
To sacrifice what humans love most:
Greed.

Dasche Ryan (12)
North Cambridge Academy, Kings Hedges

A Burning Landscape

The sky looks like a sunset,
but it's too soon.
It shouldn't be pink yet,
it is only noon.

The trees must not have grown yet,
they've no leaves or bling.
But, how could I forget?
It is already spring.

Where are the creatures?
Maybe they're in hibernation.
But this isn't nature's place,
this is domination.

Manon Turner (12)
North Cambridge Academy, Kings Hedges

When...

When a human is eating food,
animals are being eaten.

When a human is building houses,
animals are losing houses.

When a human is cooling and chilling,
animals are hot and dying.

When a human is hunting for fun,
animals are dying for nothing.

But, when a human is living a perfect life,
a human is also dying for food.

Abby Ho (12)
North Cambridge Academy, Kings Hedges

Global Inferno

The forests are burning,
The ice caps are melting,
The sea is warming,
It's getting hotter.

Fire,
It makes disasters,
Red, orange, yellow,
Endlessly blazing.

Fire creates disasters,
It spreads like plague,
Red, orange, yellow,
Endlessly blazing.

Isaac Rayson (12)
North Cambridge Academy, Kings Hedges

Young Writers Information

We hope you have enjoyed reading this book – and that you will continue to in the coming years.

If you're the parent or family member of an enthusiastic poet or story writer, do visit our website **www.youngwriters.co.uk/subscribe** and sign up to receive news, competitions, writing challenges and tips, activities and much, much more! There's lots to keep budding writers motivated!

If you would like to order further copies of this book, or any of our other titles, then please give us a call or order via your online account.

Young Writers
Remus House
Coltsfoot Drive
Peterborough
PE2 9BF
(01733) 890066
info@youngwriters.co.uk

Join in the conversation!
Tips, news, giveaways and much more!

 **YoungWritersUK** 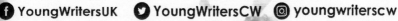 **YoungWritersCW** 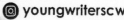 **youngwriterscw**